DATE DUE

2003

ME WITH ANIMAL TOWERING

ALBERT MOBILIO

me With Animal Towering

BLACK SQUARE EDITIONS

HAMMER BOOKS

NEW YORK

COPYRIGHT © 2002 BY ALBERT MOBILIO / ISBN 0-9712485-1-6
FIRST PRINTING MAY 2002 / DESIGNED BY QUEMADURA / GRATE-
FUL ACKNOWLEDGEMENT IS MADE TO THE FOLLOWING PUBLICA-
TIONS IN WHICH SOME OF THESE POEMS FIRST APPEARED: *HAM-
BONE, THE GERM, ANGLE, BOMB, TITANIC OPERAS* / PUBLISHED
IN THE UNITED STATES BY BLACK SQUARE EDITIONS, AN IMPRINT
OF HAMMER BOOKS, 130 WEST 24TH STREET, #5A, NEW YORK, NY
10011 / U.K. OFFICES: FOUR WALLS EIGHT WINDOWS/TURNAROUND,
UNIT 3, OLYMPIA TRADING ESTATE, COBURG ROAD, WOOD GREEN,
LONDON N22 6TZ, ENGLAND / ALL RIGHTS RESERVED / LIBRARY
OF CONGRESS CATALOGING-IN-PUBLICATION INFORMATION ON
FILE / NO PART OF THIS BOOK MAY BE REPRODUCED, STORED IN
A DATA BASE OR OTHER RETRIEVAL SYSTEM, OR TRANSMITTED
IN ANY FORM, BY ANY MEANS, INCLUDING MECHANICAL, ELEC-
TRONIC, PHOTOCOPYING, RECORDING, OR OTHERWISE, WITHOUT
THE PRIOR WRITTEN PERMISSION OF THE PUBLISHER.

CONTENTS

This structure of ideas, these ghostly sequences
Of the mind, result only in disaster. It follows,
Casual poet, that to add your own disorder to disaster

Makes more of it.

WALLACE STEVENS

"The Bed of Old John Zeller"

Only we see death; the free animal has its demise
perpetually behind it and before it always
God, and when it moves, it moves into eternity,
the way brooks and running springs move.

RAINER MARIA RILKE

"The Eighth Elegy"

FOR JENNY SCOBEL

We stroll to the tree &
when I look at her closely she
makes me tingle like I've been scrubbed

The loam on which we sit, with its
formless, singing, rudimentary
lust of earth; the breezes

slapping our faces, insects
in crevices, and mountainous premonitions
I was beginning to use

four-lettered words, to use the Public
Library, to fence-hurdle, and
clean my fingernails all the time

Whatever she was, she was
a chafed & blinkered creature, sometimes
feeling the bottom-numbness of heart

that comes with the pleasure of
issuing small commands
Her papery breath on my wrist,

& my stammering makes us such a pretty,
self-caressing sight
We hide beneath the bundled maze of leaves,

our throats burned up by our surmises
Abnormally palpable, we pass from each
to the other jumpy versions

of a conscienceless animal
As we dredge strength from causality's fix,
we hope for milk & honey & pillars of

cloud willing to interfere with sundials
She is snug in her unthreatened skin,
like a glistening rubber-stamp

freshly daubed in ink
untroubled by this darting impermanence
The two of us sitting in this clump

of flowers, crushing some, hands
pressed & variously tangled
Yes, civilization, you are a blustering,

teeth-chattering giant afraid of self-made mice,
yet we do not count ourselves among
the sexually veiled people; our invitations

are cleaner, so much more usable than
the artifices of rooms
We are regulated, least-dreaming amid

the sweet drugging of breath & our zig-
zag motions are precisely
inflicted on each body's bright graph

They threw in the towel, they burnt
the notes. The chairs were folded up, the microphone

unplugged. After the questionnaires were collected,
we mopped the linoleum floor—the sickening smears

were rubbed into ever-thinning arcs. I watched
from behind the bandstand as the Pinnacle kids

draped the Contact Mirror that hours before
had shivered under the assault of

one thousand flashlights. Another root worked
into the soil; the encirclement's nearly done.

Outside, the men smoked as their exhalations
thickened under the awning. Everywhere, the salt

smell of bodies revved up, ready to flare. Voices,
hoarse and sated, rode a damp breeze. *When the stick*

is crooked, someone said. *Our sting will then*
be felt, I sang back, each word familiar

as the sore in my mouth my tongue can't leave
alone. Cars started, headlights bit

into the gloom at this, the furthest verge,
where a cure will soon take hold.

the long & shortened
      flame is sounding, then

raised, then instantly falls. These
      experiments

soothe the reaction of the pulse.

its flutter is Curvingly
      the length of arms
especially those

near the horizon, that sometimes
    I have watched woods
        fired to clear the ground, have

seen them flash, ruby flecked
      earth
charred by watery   scars.

POP SONG

some of them found me,

& some then said,
you might
as well just stall
& dive, go perilously down
through however much
air it takes
to smash your wanting more
of this on open ground
& stay there head
too low to make a peep

then i said that i could surely
do that many times,
& even many times harder
but it would still be as if
i was here with you, my face
finding a way into yours,
while pleading all these
spilt-milk & bad-break lines,
yet knowing your listening
box is shut &
that all the heart you have
I've long since had & now lies
beaten up, unbodied,
like Liston in Miami '64

all of You go on down
   prostrate, bug-
               eyed & lovingly,

before this   Judo monster with
   seething mouth, iron dogs
   for feet & the whole   slipshod

Nation of assembly-line goof-offs for
                prehensile Paws, so fall

kneeward before the Terror that is: *having*
to be Someplace easy,   bend your

too bendable Spine at the toothy Prospect
            of a mighty long
              time

till Recess comes—or not at all 'cept
   for a failed quadruple by-pass or the M15
   bus jumping the curb

as you graze a magazine, your thoughts in far-off
                Climes
   Uncoupled from the Task,

& suddenly you're another dough-boy gone
                        face-down in Big muddy.

But other living tunes intrude. You query,
When does the air sleep? And how
            can we breath when it does?

You have to get used to the ground, daily
    contact with rocks & water
                        against those rocks;

that's Reasonable living in the Narrows,
    where no dogs howl at the jackhammering lovers

behind the window shade; no hose on them,
yet still, how Figure (why try?) the probability
            as this observable daddy

                pitches forward, head destined
to smack so solid a bedpost, then

that sudden signal in his brain: of damage,
bloodburst & maybe, sorry chum, Some sizable
                coma. Alas.

Limbs greased with fear, these cartoon creatures move
like dead leaves scurrying under storm bruised
skies; so slid upon glass

they are, you can't follow as they zing around
that roomful house, crazily pouring
themselves through a needle's eye.

As rootie-toot music wraps up another hunt my fast
twitch muscles fire in time
to the xylophones. I'm worn out

from the chase yet still unclutched
in lung-seizing air. But Christ, that mouser who died in an egg-
beater's roar, where mercy
got thrown along

with my skidding head, has surely sailed down, maybe,
for the last time. Or could it be
some rising

waits for him, a raw breath heaving
its way through wrung-out fur till somehow love's bad screw-
ing over is forgot & the world again
is nothing more   than one rat's living scent.

Misled as to the nature of your overtures, still I ended up
waking in your royal house on a bed of snow-colored leaves
to the sound of sibilant birds. In that greasy spoon off Back-
Rub Alley, I thought you meant something like *Narrate my shad-
owy past* when, in fact, you really meant nothing more than *I've
been ringside at the vocabulary wars.* Perhaps it was the liquor I'd
consumed or the cowboy-swing broadcast I was receiving in
my recent dental work, but I misunderstood. What I thought
was the unfurling of your sails was just you pulling some pa-
per towels to clean up something dirty on your blouse. Mis-
takes like this get made. Maybe I make them more than oth-
ers but that's because I think too much about why I think too
little. That is, most of the time I'm trying to shelve a few sen-
tences in my head but my mouth is selling them fast at dis-
count prices.

And this bothers me so I brood about it. And while I'm
brooding someone might blow cool air across their steam-
ing porridge, look up and fix me with expectant eyes and say
Inhabit the flower and the insect it tempts, and I would hear instead,
A cabin and an hour of sex is for rent. You can see how trouble might
spring from my preoccupation. My brain is a cheap radio
with a bent antennae and a broken dial; the reception's bad
and one station's always bleeding into another. Whatever I
hear comes in bitten-off bits, shot through with static. No,

you can't blame me when I hear wrong what you said right. When you said you *liked to drink for free*, my badly tuned head made out that you were a *dyke who would live for me*. Right after you told me to shush so I wouldn't spoil your sousing, I remember waking, those crisp leaves crackling against my skin, in that coiled house. I found myself surrounded by the sound of diligent inquiry, the insect spiel of injected dialects. It was the flush of busy veins, the pissing roar of my own talk come back to work me over.

I heard wrong because you were bending my ear. The comical canal down which vocabulation spiraled. *The sun was dodging behind wind-blown clouds.* Not mucked enough for me. *The gunner's lodging in the beehive of a well-blown clown.* You can almost see the gurgle in my electroencephalogram. What I'm thinking about is how you kiss, how you hiss. How you miss. I'm thinking you lay me down to sleep. How you lay me down in deep. How you lazily drown and weep.

The breathy, botched gist gets phoned into headquarters as rookies hitch up their predicate stunners. Time to shake-down the crook-mouths who inhale sentences like torpedo sandwiches, crust snowing down the front of our slippery shirts. That's my swirly world. Shivers the size of an all-day sucker. Allegations about the use of my abuse. You heard it all but still brought me into your loyal house. Still played me out and flayed me within an inch of disposability. I was housed in your worldly sleeves. My head in a slipcase of whispers. Mistakes got made and get made again. A gossamer of glottal stops and strums, of words spat back from fun-house mirrors. *Speak through me*, you say. *Beat truly*, I hear. I'm thinking fast as faster can. *Cheap glue in me*, my mind makes out. *Speech chewing me*, we seem to say.

SCORE THROWN THROUGH

.

This barrelhouse devotion
        even as a kernel of
            vibration readily forms

    like a string. Surfaces take up

surrounding air, the tone of a harp, a guitar,
or violin is

root of the stretching weight when filled

        with sand as a pulse as the hand
          imparts

larger stars
          on tilting
glass
     continuous and shaken

between
extinctions. Now our singing flame

is blackened, now
desirable as   possible. I am

turning, turns away

From a boat in Crowes Harbor
   this lantern, these grass-
washed ropes   revealed

every crowd. Their rules require chasing
  down

        the ashtray mouths that
       summarize my dug up,

  burnt up, glossolalic wish

alone when urged by my lower leanings,

    contrived a means to box above.
  Wheel's teeth & pinion,
worked by a handle as a greenish dial spins

  Among us, amid these, against

some wild west's
        right-handed & left
          hooking falls

  Such whistling stunts—   we grab at weed-thick

    consequence, its higher kind of white recalls
    how our days are
            being milled

pages I have tried   such science

of place. My acoustics cause
                        them to be screened
                            mentally, and I have

            been more or less
                complete.

            My German friend has trouble reading

my natural, inevitable abrasion, so I round off
                            what cleanly
                        can be rounded off

once   Bodies were placed in deadening
          action—*we hydrogenate the voice*—

     to restage the Big Push inland over steeply
                                        made tones.

                 Lo, in sound village & self-willed
          Church, a temperature changes,

a timetable limits my deepest,

          as night's lone sirens row lengths through
                              asphalt-buckling heat

wire is plucked &

    the point is plain. You are

now in a condition to say,

how strange it seems that always your discipline
is numerous.

    Even the aided ear has to bend

to find rooms as they mingle. I will show

you my Fragmento-action upon your

       arm & ask

"what assemblage am I with," then roam another

      fundamental groove

the true physical
        air being proved to be a psalm

  saying that two mouthpiece
beats   multiplied by them-
           selves

            would
scatter toy trucks & fold our Glide god's downtown scene.

This syndrome rushes past, scarce lift against
        which   orbits stray, buttons tear &
                        a song lays
                 down its head

I am always up here & you

forget how high up from the street it is.
But I am always up here

where there are east, west & southern
scenes, there are bridges & incoming
flights from numerous

elsewheres & outgoing flights going right back.
Yet I am mostly

up here just like you used to be, or even
as you could be now if you came by
for a glass of seltzer or a smoke

by the big window, us looking that long
way down, palms brushing over an ashtray.

Jets criss-cross above the watertanks & grease-

blackened exhaust fans
smear airdraft's brakeless passage;

this snug room with its miles-deep walls
is a stone mouth we squeeze thru
into cavernous sky.

Do you remember how sharp the TV reception is
up here? No ghosts when you can almost reach

out & strum the Big Antennae; the visual
waves break & spoil somewhere
downstairs but way up

here it's static-free panoramas, pistoling
glare, the purities, etc.

So come on by, climb up
anytime & we can throw open windows

& tilt ourselves out over a birds-eye
view (like we did on the Garden Wall's slippery
cleft). We'll take Atlas-turns shouldering blue

yonder's heft, while one of us ducks
back in for coffee, coffee-

cake, the good milk & something warm to wear.
Flicking matches, we can watch their smoke

trails snake back upward even as
their twisted paper bodies fly while mostly falling.

AFTER-ESQUE

Spatial awareness expands. That awareness is never so dense as when it is the awareness of nothing in particular. **HENRI MICHAUX** *Exploring Hallucinogens*

All the bang-about worlds we knew
  just left. Packed up their silverware, trauma

rooms, satellites,   & 30-day offers, gave us
      a wink then made
         for a waiting curbside car.

So what's for us to pick at, pluck or strum upon? What's
        left? Just shadow's acreage
        sucked down
        by black eyes
        deep as drains. We root

around like kids hungering after broken Cheerios
  at the bottom of a spent box.   For years we filed away

the threats, wore ourselves out playing Coy Pretender.
  Now we're stuck within a homeless

sound that peels across what used to be the horizon—
        a wooden bell   rung in fallow air.

Some keep up the front. They hum Mancini or scuff through
wet grass the way you once could in sneakers. They talk
        the old talk

      but *long gone* are the only words we truly
        need in these, our daily   newborn days.

Send me down the old Yaloo. Maroon me off among green seas. From the few words I've said and hand gestures I've made, it's clear I'm ready to undergo my fate. No more book-ish days with my head buried in the stone cistern of gibber-jabber. Or sticky tantrums over who gets to lick the spoon. I'm done with the Suction Masquerade and my portals are cleared for a cold-blooded bath. This is where I am in the game: midway between being a pink-skinned suckling and being salted and dried like a Slim Jim ripe for idle consump-tion in the check-out line. It is, as they say, a magic moment and one that requires it's own stage directions. Flick on the smoke machines, cue the odor of a bar-brawl. The lighting should make you think of torpid afternoons—make it milky gray, the color of an old pillow. Then wheel me onstage twisted up in sheets, looking like a hand-rolled cigarette ready to have my head lit with a match. Now unfurl me on a diving board poised over a thimble. I'm a shallow water swimmer at home in a bead of sweat.

Watch my vivid plunge, my lazy backstroke, the rippled halo around my head. Out among the azure shoals tiny-waisted girls braid each other's hair with shells as I drift by. Mouths sputter bits of mango as they laugh and sing their wiry genius. I bid them adieu as the rolling surf carries me on-ward, out beyond the sound of my own breathing and self-delusion's tick-tock. The night sky is a dark slope down which I have fallen; the waves beneath me feel like a Buick Electro-Lux convertible. *At last*, I say out loud to the void, *the unfuckable totality of being.* Mouth gaping, some brine invades and I begin to cough and thrash. For a moment, out there, too far out to simply bite my lip and wake, there's a smothered roar, like the sound of a jet engine churning through my cotton-stuffed head. A deep octave groan. The sound of emergency. Of psychological readiness and task distribution. Suddenly, I am attuned to fresh possibilities. I am spitting and kicking to beat the band. Face down in black water, I begin, not lazy but hard, to do the American crawl.

have you wanted to pet these   ?

leather-bound pearls. in my monster-Sized south,
which weez looking down upon so as
to see just how far of a drop   till *never to*
                             Be found.

or have they Given us our trial & sexual Error?

my normality needs to get better, maybe even
bigger; it requires explicit instructions
                      & pressurized fluids.

do you feel the historical shrinkage of Love's teeth?

hers, her mother's, then the ones stowed away in the fear-
    box   & all of them now hardly anything
                more than graven Indentations in
                        my left calf.

so can we please ourselves with: the genuine (even if
      limited by so much demand)?   can   we squeeze
                        out of misalliance into
                something more persuasively alone?

Able in his upper parts, he is the spoon in such big
spins; he revolves like a pilot
of veiled debate. During boyhood games
a bullet tore his breastplate,
a steely arm slipped through
the bright doorway—on both cheeks kissed,
and, well, it is inevitable enough. He ruins

himself among the lowest rabble, their hand-made
lettering spreads across his stomach,
but they cannot be saddened, not
as much as his dark face
with its familiar high forehead and angular
mustache. A gurgling voice droning
in weak light; a fabled tuft of steam

drifts above the gables and domes.
Where did he hear his own
sound put into words? In a tapestried ballroom,
or deep in Clorox-scented snow?
A stranger wears a sweater dense
with physical fear, her eyes turned inward,
her waxy face too cold to notice

how dutiful his touch could be. Such
a relief for him to be alone. Books had brought

him to Europe where there was ice on the cobbles.
He wanted everything to go on
for years and years: the drumming thunder,
the lips slightly, slightly parted.
A strand of her hair contains within it the violent

potion of a prisoner's brain. *I pity them now,*
I pity us. In obscure kitchens each of them
feasts upon the snail of destiny, then exercises
the power to feign. All his great seriousness
was something on a pavement, was propped
beneath billowing awnings. With an animal's badge
affixed to his breast, he plunges headlong

toward an obedient, churning flock.
The very next evening he boards another bus
as his smooth metal fish thrashes in all
directions, its tail buttering the sun.
In a new consciousness, he remembers
her saying, *there will be sacrifice.*
He licks his fingers and lays down

upon the carpet until the finale.
It seems an illusion that these childish hands
could locate such emotions.
Yet he listens, the notes a kind of kindling.
By the sly river and its leafy bank
his compulsions swarm. And still, even among us,
he pretends to luminous sleep.

SLACK KEY AUBADE

As the raised-up sun knuckles down to business,
    as dirty trees bloom on my same, same streets,

as a congeries of worms, potato bugs & centipedes
    dig & feed in those small patches of soil

the sidewalk affords, (& all this is done to my mind's
    grindhouse piano accompaniment),

I weigh out my possible number of nexts,
    you know, next breath, next shiver-making joy,

next boozy dash of sublime disregard for a world
    peopled by assholes,

and then, as integers pile into sums, & sums sum up,
    something particular, almost molecular

takes place in the air around my face: a liquefaction,
    a thickening so sudden I feel I've been slapped by

an incoming breaker, my throat at once a salty choke. Sure,
    I exaggerate but that's self pity: bringing a temple down

around unhearing ears. I mean, we are nobodies with the Master,
    (or is it *without* him, I'm not sure), but either way

we're nobodies; we're what's called population. So please
    just shove your self-esteem, your authenticity & self-

sacrifice for that numbing buzz of others. Come live, instead
    in this cloud o' mine, my smoky *mitteleuropa* of cooked

pigeons, Panzer tracks in snow, the tin warble of *Greensleaves*
    on Armed Forces Radio & bonfires waning on the quay:

my jerrybuilt nostalgia for a Late Show movie watched
    in an Atlantic City hotel, sleepless in starch-stiff sheets,

maybe thirty years ago. But today it's this ringing heat & I can't
    breathe or think; my brain's gone slippery with the force

of these too loving blows. As the hunter sun dines
    on another fistful, as the worm revolves

around my blaze of *nexts*, as the hive quiets, and
    hope's doughy tranquilizers hit their mark

a wreath of praise deserved settles around my many
    times saved yet somewhat always broken neck.

I was alone and sad because of a recent break-up. And, I suppose, I was more than a little desperate. The woman in the apartment next door let a pretty friend from Texas stay in her apartment while she went on a weekend trip—we were introduced in the hallway at our adjacent doors. That night around 2 AM, I heard her come home and I sprang out of bed to spy through the peephole as she disappeared into the apartment. But, as I headed back into bed, she knocked. A chill slithered through my stomach. After tugging on my jeans, I opened the door. "Do you have any pot?" she asked with a drawl that curled around my head like the scent of peaches in summer. Not only did I have marijuana, I told her, but I had some cocaine. She nearly trilled, her voice sounding like the bright clang of divine scales tipping in my favor.

When we were both cozily airborne the talk turned to architecture. (She was, it turned out, an architect, like my neighbor.) I started getting out my architecture books, flipping through pages, and talking and talking for maybe two hours about the Flatiron Building, tenement design, and how she had to see the only Louis Sullivan building in New York. No, I'm not an architect. No profession at all, except maybe that of Explainer. Of course, eventually her eyes began to register the lateness of the hour and the letdown of the stimulants. "I should go," she said, no less sweetly than when she had knocked, but now all promise of delight wrung free of her lilt. She left. I reshelved my books and shuffled toward bed, my buzz having dissolved into an agitating sizzle. Me, Joe Architect. At one point I had piled three books in her lap.

The next night I cleaved to the door and sure enough she came home from clubbing at 2 AM again. Only this time she wasn't alone. She shushed his booming voice while fishing for keys. I screwed my eye into the peephole and watched them, their heads swollen and gleaming in the magnifying glass, as they stumbled tipsily through her door. Even after the door slammed shut audible gusts of boozy joy still rose and fell from what I could (no, *couldn't* help but) imagine to be some playful rite of flirtation and undress. Soon enough, though, the sounds ceased.

I sat down on my couch, smoked a leftover roach and began watching an infomercial about body hair removal. As the familiar lofting took hold around my head, I remembered she had asked me, "Why do you know so much about design?" I had paused for a long, awkward moment. It was still early in my spiel; I could have stopped. She had just shed her shoes to tuck her feet under her legs. But I didn't. I had more talking to do. Couldn't she see? I was the Master Builder.

The imaged Word, it is, that holds
Hushed willows anchored in its glow.

HART CRANE

"Voyages, VI"

so go)

So go cremator. And hobnobbing hobs thusly.   These Flight
removals, they're clannish. They took to me
like whatever takes to water. While: we remaining were

bumped from how, then simply said the mind   Falls back.
    falls otherward, then   looses its tune.

tilted)

Not enough shut-eye makes pater bald by Towel light. Nearly
sifted who from him? OK, it's just   some presence

on a good Wood floor which fades. I'm with you on this One
because others I've missed & miss me they do too. Like supper,
    left on

the little oblong dish.   The mercy's mild that way,

guzzling Waves then groans. Our panacea.   Playing the
police as they pull up a chair, and wonder Which. & wonder
    with.

house holds)

Big deal. Pillow sale for them. How they tied up, rode groovy
into Bitetown. Vroom, vroom. Such miracle love as. Notes,
    kickbacks, &

    disturb: ing lubrication. It's funny now in retro but when we

were in it, right in it, we Felt squeezed. Did You? Or does you
only do luv & kisses?   We got tasty tablets to take

upon this rock with sending sky.
Returning world.   oh, yeah. Could be big, should a bowie
    knife Round
    us out. I'm living within my flaking

paintjob's room   yet still Clue & covet a Greyhound zone.

faintly strum)

Come sound. Sped up thru twisted slides. My joke, your Works,
your Days. They are so much warmer, particular

and rung.   Your secessionists restored me. From a sunken
    standoff
where arrows, pikes, nails

bloodied the air. *Dear, dear.* How null the non has
    gotten since I kept. A lovely old. Our lonesome, roaring bone.

the slang)

The conversation turns. Famished and wishing, I'm willing
   to give it
a few weeks. Call me semi-
estranged.   Or eat half & toss the rest.

He's typical. So's me too. Insofar as book-length, boldfaced
excitation goes. My Episode went off

without a hitch.   They clubbed the start, of *please begin*.
And now who's got the poetry Power?   To do

what needs be done.   When the phone is bitter
as it is held.   As no position I'm in   to complain about
getting frisked by baby's fingerToys.

swerves to turn)

Then seek this path. Torn ship, holy
    pope in Ropetown.   Steer into this face that is:

Sunk in cosmographic Thrills or gone for its furtive
                    smoke behind a salty pillar, where
a greasy look can be thrown at heaven's Sly descender.

I swerve away from. All those goosey truths & ask:

Where are ye, nymphs
           amid   such bitched-out noise?

more plot)

Smash beds and smash the chalice lore. Sweet del Debbie
    sew.n like a flag
on my teenage scene. The second

she's back, we dress.   What else
can the mower mow down now? That evening

got all drawed over with Crayons, leaving me
    the news that, hey, the   shelter slice is Ready.

chemical revs)

Still. Steady, able to roam you. What an individual earns

in the absence of common rules. This is why you can
disregard or.   This is why you can be deep. And

that's why the importance fizzes over. With which we feel
    found. By

watching Intelligent movies, the ones They watch. The ones
    I'll try to show you.   Then tow my Corrected crown
                        down to formaldehyde dumps.

the truces)

Whether we booze broadly. Persepolis quakes, the laundry
lists. And thereupon we heap ourselves up as

idiot stones are heaped up under a succession. Of skies.
    By Muscular
arms of the ancients.   Their solutions.   All, *all*
solved. The versions mine.   They had taken to calling

me noonish. Or spoonly done. Calling me incalculate. Per voice.
    Some wind-up gadget you use instead of.

A bony boy named *Inkstick*
    published these radical tears.   The deep trances & card
tricks. What's solid onstage, isn't off.   So he left your

meal with the dogs. Then you were close enough to see the ear

is   pink so what you say is meant   to be sensual.   Pliable,
antidote-wise. Could deft mind thus characterize?

a camera bathes us)

Voice-over at the ice show. An audience craving audacity.
   Craved brackish drink. And the best
of the bad.   You see, they wanted the Low-down

on the verbal,   maybe the medieval, who. Knows.   But this
   ding-dong
daddy is Said to be from Dumas. He says we size to fit.

My globe   Tucked between the halves. Shit weather for
the Girlgang spectacular. Why did we headlong clash? All our
   skin, another
detonation once   we uncovered the switch.

Go slow, mr. mercury, you have steeped me in your house.

my gown)

Is it true? Is this true? The way this is. It's uncut & cruelly
brought around. The idea of rearmament gains.   Additional

fans. Tony Curtis as Iago in *Othello: Black Commando*,
    such a skinny brute dressed in such alarming aerials.

No matter, he's my tool, my sketch. Gone since,   I don't smoke
those antsy things
anymore. Just fibrilla.tion. But only   enough to quit.

My lungful, my idolatries. Souls
    harvested & shouldered: mere medical manipulation.

partly stuttered slide)

Sure it was so. We was stone
& dirty lore. We was at Rigolettos. Our ruminated bodies
less dense.   Than air. Therefore,

hung up on those keepsake gradations. You know,
Polaroid-bleary resemblances to the Steady,
        acutely Mindful mind.   Switch

allegiances to *My Tribe's Idols*, they'll never
        slag you in the trenches, boy. You can relax, be

King of Mints, all right.   And if you get stunned
                by high Purpose you're a goner
                        anyways, however sweetly, shyly you.

chaining)

Give her some time. All along, she meant. Such relief once
    necessary,
now caught in basement pipes. Caught in tightly mades. From
    air-raid church to.

My grease-cake idyll. Thems so specific
in her wake. Theys home in a Rising rhythm. And me

working this hand-me-Down abbreviator. Our first impulse
was, well, wrong. A disaster.   In our sexual bigtop, we roast
    within.

The intimacy of the long room seen
shriveled, Translucent. Her   flavor flown. Shaved
down. I'm peaking, sharp as ever. Behind   as well as   begun.

then deftly)

And my hut is designed to collapse. So as to Shift from this

tricky Part. To blastproof doors. Let's hook into what's
    doing down
in the process garage. My krazy-kat high jinking will

boost morale among the disassembly Boys. No credible
scenario, no sulphurous pit.   A concrete squad lines us
up against the looming. roller.   They palm me, bunkerlike,

as if mere Curvature could make my false life
somehow   more like true.

Can high. Guidance be
        the wing for us?   Please, traveler,   Say.

In parochial school the nuns would stand RIGHT BEHIND the boys as we queued up at the urinals. The aptly named Tom Pretty once spun around and wagged his pubescent yet marvelously free-form wang at Sister Lucinda—a withered 70 year-old who appeared to be nothing so much as a skeleton wrapped in wet paper—and hissed, "If ya wanna see it so bad, then here it is!" As his cackle played off the green-tiled walls we warily peeked up from our own tasks to see what she would do. She showed no reaction. In fact, she seemed to stare through him, to a place somewhere outside the confines of the lavatory. He was not disciplined. Lately I have found myself thinking about him. Has he been successful in life, or met with disappointment? Does he feel he was bestowed with great license or that he was burdened with great debt? Mostly, though, I wonder if he has retained his enviable faith in the spontaneous overflow of powerful feelings.

AIRPROOF

FOR HELMUT FEDERLE

There is nothing in the air. No whispers combed by branches. No premonitions of change. No birds on the wing. The facts of its molecular composition aside, the air is nothing; the nothing we know intimately. The air is empty of anything but itself, and this, in a way, is a pure kind of emptiness. Were you to open a door into a room filled only with air, you would still call it empty. But, having opened that door and found the room empty, you might find yourself perplexed, perhaps suspicious of the lack of furnishings. You might then say, "There's something in the air" by way of voicing your sense of something imminent. Of something odd about to happen. But there is, in truth, nothing in the air. Rather, it's the emptiness of air which registers on your pulse. The something in the air you feel is the palpable consequence of there being nothing but air.

Let's say you step into this room, the small room filled only with air. You immediately sense its walls closing in around you. At once, this room seems airless and even though the room is empty it is experienced as full, too full to accommodate you and your need for air. You might then formulate a plan to uncrowd this room in which there is, in fact, nothing. You will "air out" the room. Strangely, to air out the room you must bring more air in. Bringing in more air by opening a window doesn't make the room fuller—the actual quantity of air doesn't change, only its quality—but instead makes it feel more spacious. You can breathe more easily. You drink in the air, and begin to gauge yourself a bit smaller: by swallowing nothing you enlarge its potential scope outside of you while your shrinking body collapses upon the void which you've inhaled. You are a vessel into which the room, the world, empty the emptiness of air.

As the room fills with more air, fresher air, air from outside, once again you conclude there's something in the air. Trees, the damp bark's scent, decaying leaves. The season's change. The progression of the calendar. Your own mortality. All of these things are suddenly, piercingly in the air. Yet there's really nothing in the air. The air is the same as it was—the same mix of countless molecules—although its proportions have shifted ever so slightly. But the air is the same empty air as it was before you opened the window. A micro-fraction more of sulfur dioxide or chlorophyll does not constitute mortality. Mortality is not in the air. The nothing that is in the air is not mortal; it has always been there. Even before the molecules that make up the air congealed sufficiently to be something called air, there was a limitless lack awaiting its form, its signifier.

Walk outside this once airless room to breathe deeply and you are said to "take the air." As you draw air into your lungs, you do not diminish the amount of air around your head, across the street, or in Sacramento. The sum of air is fixed.

Indeed, the air cannot be "taken" anywhere since it is everywhere. And if you could take it, scoop out a palmful, the place of that air, the air pocket, would be instantaneously filled by the air around that place. You cannot make an empty place in emptiness. The air's emptiness is everywhere at once; it is an imperial emptiness. Yet it remains bound by its nature: The air cannot escape itself. Conversely, we cannot escape the air. You sleep in it, you inhale it; when you are happy, you are thought to "walk on air." The space you occupy is only "you" to the extent it is *not* air, not emptiness. We are airlocked and, perhaps, in this imprisoned condition, we grow airsick. There is nothing in the air and some of that nothing we feed to our blood. It envelopes something there inside us, the thing that isn't in the air, the thing called mortality. The air is not mortal yet it insistently gloves the whole of our perishable selves. It delineates our presence as thoroughly as its empty eternity smothers us. There is nothing in the air. Except you, pushing through it, open-mouthed, empty-handed. Breathing nothing, breathing air.

ARGONAUTEN

FOR MAX BECKMANN

So I guess you could say I'm living one of those Daddy-Don't-Bite-You'll-Leave-a-Bruise lives down here in Redondo Beach, the kind of life a gal like me ends up with when you're born craving everybody's eyes on you. You know, the girl who never wants to take off her First Communion dress, who grows up wanting something to wash off Baltimore's crab cake stink. I came to Los Angeles in '54 and earned myself a couple of showboat years. Walk ons, and half a page of lines in *Hell Canyon Outlaws*. I did a funny bit with Don Knotts in *No Time for Sergeants*. Along the way there were some dinners at Chasens and Brown Derby, even if sneaking leftovers in my purse wasn't the glamorous thing to do. For a while I even dated Dore Schary's right-hand guy. But by '62 even small parts got harder and harder to come by. Suddenly you're too old, hips too big, lips too thin, circles under the eyes too dark to cover up without laying on the pancake with a putty knife. Hell, mostly you're just too much of a reminder, the bad stomach after you were a tasty meal, and you can't compete with the pigtail nieces from good schools back East, or this month's babydoll, or one of those up-and-comin' strivers who will nuzzle your lap while riding in a convertible down the coast highway. Afterwards, she won't insist on being driven home but instead is glad to take cab fare and a drop off in Santa Monica.

These days it's the same raft of wheedlers selling you a shot at some glitter only these guys haven't been buffed up with movie swag. You know the type, tape on their glasses and Ban-Lon pants. And the new deal is I've got to do in front of the camera what I used to do to get there. For some girls that's a big difference and I guess I thought it would be for me too. Until I did a shoot. When it was done I felt about the same as I used to after a night of doing time as some studio clown's arm jewelry and realizing, when I finally shut my apartment door behind me, that I'd lost my garter snaps in his car. In other words, it's no big deal. They're called smokers, skinflicks, blue movies. Whatever you call them, it's the same old bang around about a sailor boy and some stockings, a push-up bra and a little cha-cha-cha. Christ knows, you're acting. Acting to beat the band, like when you're getting your behind paddled with a tennis racket while you twist and howl like somebody's set your bum on fire. Getting something like that to look good ain't a piece of cake; you have to work at it. Make it swing to make it look real. Sometimes I use a toothbrush on my neck and cheeks to give me a sex flush. It shows up fine in black and white. And I came up with a neat trick for bondage bits—I rub Vaseline on the clothesline so I can squirm and twist without getting rope burn. Little things like that make for what they call job satisfaction. The real payoff is still what I came out here for in the first place—getting everybody's eyes dead on me. I'm up there, maybe not hitting the bigtime, but still up there in front of wide eyes. Up there on bed sheets and backwalls in

American Legion Halls, frats, grindhouses, and bachelor pads from Catalina to the Chesapeake. I mean nobody's going to mistake me for Blanche DuBois, but it's still showbiz. Thrashing my hair and panting like a choo-choo train, I'm still in pictures.

Photo modeling doesn't pay as much but it's an easier day. Last summer I did jungle girl and nudist camp shoots for *Tab* and *Photoplay*. You know, gobs of cleavage, bikini behinds, and nothing too naughty. For the dirty bookstore stuff, I go up to Venice to this guy who has a big double garage. He rents maybe a half room of used furniture and presto, you've got a set. Whether its monkeypod chairs or fancy old couches with fringe, he tells you what he's got the day before so you can pick out the clothes to go with the mood. See, you wouldn't wear an orange two-piece to sit on a brocade sofa. You might go for some kind of old-fashioned type nightie or an evening dress. Something indoorsy. Not too California. With wicker chairs and throw rugs you might dress up more fun and sunny. Once I did a panty layout with a guy in Van Nuys where he wanted me in a Donna Reed outfit—wool skirt, little pillbox hat—and most of the shots were of me bending over and lifting my skirt while I stood in front of a kitchen table all set for breakfast. The photographer was a sweet, wiry-haired guy who talked the whole time about different structural designs for girdles and bras. Very technical stuff about lift, stress and drag. He knew all the foundation garment companies and had his favorites. One reason I feel safe with these guys is because they're so damn serious about all this. They're not hounds sniffing after you; instead they're all nervous and finicky like they're getting ready for the big history test tomorrow. They're too busy having you tug your skirt up and down an inch till they can get just the right bit of behind to show. It's almost cute sometimes, like the breakfast fellow, who turned red in the face when he asked me to squeeze the Electro-Perc between my legs.

Mostly what I do is pretty tame, but you have to understand that's the original party girl talking. For me, posing isn't much different from the jobs a lot of my girlfriends do, you know, being a typist or a waitress. You can work for jerks in any business. But I don't take work that doesn't look like fun. So when the Venice shutter-bug put a painter friend of his on to me and the guy calls and the first thing he asks is, *Do you have an ass that could launch a thousand ships*, well I don't miss a beat and I say, *It's an ass that will float your boat.* I tell him, *Me and it get cash up front, 4 hours minimum, and if you don't like that you can kiss it goodbye.* He made a smooch sound and said, *Hey that's fine, bring it along with you.* I figured he was a good bet. He told me he had a costume but asked if I could get sandals. So a week later I'm squatting on top of a Greek warrior mask holding what felt like an 80 pound sword. A girlfriend of mine who did makeup on that Jason and the Argonauts movie loaned me a beat up pair of leather thong sandals. They were as comfortable as claws, but then again what would a Greek nymph do in a pair of stiletto heels. All day this guy went on about growing up in East New York, how he pitched pennies on street corners and loved egg creams. Sometimes the listening is the only really embarrassing part of this work. We'd break for ice tea and then I had to hoist up that damn sword again. He wanted me topless for awhile and then for awhile I wore my bra. He ended up painting me with the bra on, but he made it look like an ancient Greek bra, you know, made out of cowhide or something. I don't know if they even had bras back then. He probably didn't either. I think he got most of his ideas from Hercules movies. He did tick me off once when he used the word "knockers." Maybe I do dirty pictures, and maybe I've got a nasty mouth on me, but I still appreciate a gentleman.

Anyhow, I made a very nice dime for the day and the guy took a picture of the finished painting, which I put on my bureau. Obviously, there's not much of my posing that blends easily into home decoration. I do keep some of the stuff though, my best shots, in a trunk under the bed even though I worry that, Jesus, if something happens to me, my mother will be out here from Baltimore going through it. That's a big reason why I'm such a careful driver. In the painting my breasts aren't showing and I'm kinda glad about that, although, God knows, they've been out to play everywhere else. But this is different. It reminds me of high-school drama class when I was Caesar's wife. Or of being in Greece, where I've never been, but still it makes me think I have. It gets me wondering about calling some agents again. It's been years since I sat around wishing I was Jayne Mansfield but maybe I could do character stuff. Not that I mind giving an occasional coffee pot a squeeze. I like having a good laugh and making somebody out there taste that laugh. I mean, they've really got to *taste* it. But the weird thing about the painting is that it makes *me* taste something. A metal taste, like you get just before the big drop on the roller coaster over on Santa Monica Pier. When I see me as that warrior gal, the hair on my neck stands up. I think it might be a kick if she took her top off and shimmied for the Greeks. I'm close to her for a moment and the here and now slips to the end of a long skinny string. Then the tickle on my neck starts to bite. That's when I almost say out loud, *Honey, no matter what, don't you ever let go of that sword.*

When the gunships lit on the basketball courts
the Filipino grocer took hold of a Duraflame log

with one hand then palmed a cantaloupe in the other
as if batting practice were about to begin under

a sky whose stitches had been torn out so it could
be refitted for a fatter, meaner sun. They touched

down on the asphalt, sucking up a sandstorm of
Popsicle sticks, gum wrappers & grit. Marvelously

armed, with rockets at midships and armor-piercing
canons mounted at the helm, those whirlybirds

bristled like pissed-upon hornets. Tomatoes and bell
peppers fluoresced under their spiky glare,

while our grocer's for-the-fences swing smacked hell
out of a melon. Mealy shreds of rind only scattered

in the bus lane but those big guns started
strumming anyway. She wore hip-

huggers, this kid who skipped between the fancy
blooms of smoke. She navigated loosely, outstretched

arms whipsawing as she danced past him being dragged
across the playground, heels in one long bloody scuff.

Still, he managed to cock an ear to catch
her earrings' swishy jangle. *She's a natural*, he sang back

over his shoulder, as the big bird's door closed
behind him, *She's a natural spark transmitter.*

A body undergoes death when the proportion of motion and rest which obtained mutually among its several parts is changed.

When a body, which goes under among the mutually changed, is obtained, death of proportion rests its several parts and motion.

Several of the parts, among which a motion mutually rests, obtained proportion when death undergoes its body and is changed.

Death is a changed motion which, when obtained, undergoes several parts of the body and rests mutually among its proportions.

Among several parts of proportion, which changed when obtained, the rest is death and its motion goes mutually under a body.

Parts changed and a motion undergoes the death of rest, which is obtained when its body mutually parts among several.

And a body is changed when, obtained among several motions mutually, the proportion of its rest which parts undergoes death.

Of obtained death and, mutually, its several body parts, rest is a proportion which undergoes motion when among the changed.

Mutually, proportion is changed among the death of several, and its rest obtained when a body motion, which goes under, parts.

Several changed when a body, which is motion, undergoes and mutually proportions the rest of its death among obtained parts.

Rest, which a body undergoes, is its death when, mutually, proportion parts among several of the obtained and changed motions.

Mosquitoes in the mind. O what a druggy war
we fought. What we conquered was a cloud
that stumbles; what we spoke

through was a glittering flute. Our slender
fire was doused, then boxed
for easy handling. Beneath the pines

and knee-deep in the grass, the whirring
sound of airborne birth. A high mental
shadow arrives as an angel might, swiftly

peeling the lid off the sky. Whatever
was cast off is now provisional: something
more said than seen. Remember how

the cairns appeared? Piled up, an altar
on asphalt, nearest the Stop 'n Shop exit.
They knocked us loopy in the lot, snared

our ears with traffic all around,
small mouths feeding on small nouns.
Somehow we learned: The strong do

what they must, the rest live underwritten
plots. Mosquitoes skim
the mind, dry needles underfoot.

Each muscle's twitch is an infraction
against the nun who rules still air. Nothing
doing in the branches; the heat's

too much for crows. We talk with
underwater voices, loud enough to be heard
over lamplight's roar,

but tuned so they can handily
snatch fire from a candle's lip. By sending
decoys out from brittle nests, we imply

ourselves by increments—sluggish tongues
and sandbagged eyes—then make
a languorous music

out of worn down expectations.
To cloak ourselves in a bower of ready
bliss, we'll hang tough in the left-hand turn lane,

then sink low within hollow darkness,
unpatterned by love, spit or idiot hope,
a leafy, unmade bed in which no one ever lies.

The Pharaohs were lost. Woebegone and intricately lost. They sipped diet soda and contemplated their situation. They had lived within the language of a sky-heavy land and now the blackboard was wiped clean. Nothing to say and no one who would understand them anyway. The Pharaohs kept a sparse place: a canvas sling chair, a pillow sofa, some milk crates for bookshelves, and a framed poster showing a train engine steaming out of a fireplace. There were some candles and a Mexican bowl sat on the kitchen counter. Carved ibis birds, some reeds, and stacked sarcophagi could be found in the den. It was a neatly kept ranch house in a newer part of town. On the fridge, stuck under a plastic watermelon magnet, was a clay tablet with information about an orthodontia appointment for one of the kids. In the foyer hung a lacquered plaque which read, "God created me to do what he wished done, and my perfection is remembered by means of his temple."

The big sadness, the one that went unmentioned, like a bad smell in a cabinet under the sink, was how once they'd been Lords of Egypt and now, well, they weren't. Guests just ignored the fall from grace. Occasionally somebody might say something reminiscent of a forsaken past: Someone might say, "Social security is just another pyramid scheme." Or, "Did you ever watch $20,000 Pyramid?" Or, "Hey, Sphinxface, get your fingers out of my burrito!" The Pharaohs did their best not to react. Maybe you would catch a downcast eye, a forlorn yet regal sigh, but otherwise they put up a good front. Most folks were only vaguely aware that they had been more than a few rungs up the ladder from the rest of us. That the desert sun once rose from their hearts and the Nile had flowed from their breasts. That the Kingdom of the Dead was their eternal domain. If the jewels that had been their eyes had long since been hacked out by blasphemous robbers, they never complained. With us they were happy to chat about school zoning and the dog that keeps overturning the recyclables containers. Never got snooty and dropped names like Osiris or Horus. The Pharaohs, shorn of their divine essence, dispossessed of their throne, and cast out among scabrous multitudes, were good neighbors. And they would let you borrow their carved ivory knives for dinner parties.

On summer nights we sometimes sit with them out on the patio and listen to their collection of old 78s on a vintage Victrola. They love the Mills Brothers and Billy Eckstine. When dark settles in and the kids are off chasing lightning bugs across the lawn, they might open up a bit. Their talk can turn wistful. Memories are unearthed from the humid air: Apis, the sacred bull of Memphis, Wadjet, the cobra goddess of Buto, or the royal tombs at Abydos. A gazelle's hoof might be pulled from a fringed leather pouch. The lore of the long dead given breath. So many good days now gone. Beer warms in our glasses and the moon sharpens the edges of great fists of clouds. "Cab driver once more round the block," the Mills Brothers harmonize, the singing suddenly intruding on the conversation. Then the Pharaohs grow quiet, lost in thought, as an empire of bright dust settles in their eyes.

He was relieved to discover. Then his mind
moved on. He took the long view
and never tired of hearing.
It was unwise to shift his glance from
her deliberate, plaintive way.
No delight could disturb her. Puzzled
though, that the music
had stopped. It was impossible to keep
his mind on adding figures. A few
brisk shakes. Her true plateau,
its eccentricities. And tomorrow
everyone would know.

He was telling what things would be like.
He looked wretchedly embarrassed
and drew circles. He struggled with
a dizzy sort of incredulity. Secretly he felt it.
Dots and dashes of that winter.
Another year, when things were quieter.
The night air was fresher.
There was a word, mobility. An awkward
word. He could move her either up
or down or just sit there. Something needed
to be finished and hands changed.
Impersonal and bare, a readable script.

He knew he should not show it. He took
a swallow. Possessed of a different
mind about her, he glanced back.
Before he said anything
more, he checked. It was the windless noise
of small, lapping waves. She asked
if they might walk out there and see.
It was one of the most beautiful questions
that anyone had ever asked him. They were
crossing. Something humdrum. Indelible.
The tension had eased. Fathoms deep,
but its echoes were still with him.

He was thinking it sounded
innocent and artificial. There was no sign
of life, not even a trace of. It's always
harder talking when you know, she said.
A slanting moon. Without
speaking, they stood for a moment listening.
He liked to imagine himself fully trained.
If things had been just slightly
different. It was almost as if she had never
happened, but not quite. His mind was
elsewhere, and someday. A conversation
they would carry, they could call their own.

Let's get married. Bites, bruises. The usual gifts. We'll subject ourselves to wearisome bouts of meta-fiction. We'll dance the populist remedy. I'll play the woodsy loner and you can dress up like his toothpick-splitting sister. After some damp imponderables on the old couch, the familiar groove in one another's brain will play. I want to shadow you on crutches. Bend beneath your prow. You can apprentice as my nimble handler, wearing pearl-gray gloves and your rough-road slouch. Think of me as the darling son you gave away, the shepherd boy who tends your pretty lambs. Investigate my compulsions, my need to wear my affection as if it was a skin-tight shirt, or the way I require your vigilant eye on my undressed elation. I will swallow your river of half-truths and sweat lies for you to taste. I want to pronounce whatever feral words your tongue can't make its way around, to smoke the residue that collects in your quarrels. We will mark the hours on one another's clock. We will cave in on each other's mine.

The bodily instruments have been put to the whetstone; our sanctities are polished and ready for servitude. Our lamentations mingle in our basement lair. We're the six-week-running winning couple on American Bandstand taking a slow number, say, Eddie Holman's "Hey There Lonely Girl." My pompadour is an ancient relic in 1969, yet the Bandstand kids forgive me because, watching us sway, they know you do. You are the distance I must crawl across before I can dine at instinct junction. Let's get married and gather our powers. Cook our contagion. More fingers into fists than kisses into kindling. An immolation of hex-stoked limbs. We'll run like hungry dogs among fruitful vines, teeth slick from whatever pulpy thing catches our eye. We'll be slaves to neurological accident; fugitives from the mighty arrow. Let's accept our ropy dosage and go do what tired voices do, let's wither down to a rasp. We'll throw a party where everyone rolls back their head to feed their face to the sun's brash flare. We'll serve sand in fancy glasses. And our wedding keepsake will be the tough and dirty mouth that comes from trying to cheat a thirst.

This is the hand that works all these

circulatory tubes and wires
This is what handles slowly the dial

of explication which bears me along
and along again
Another slave to the mentality spree

hangs his head among us—a rose glass
fills with fingerprints he left behind
Later, wind tears the streets of Broom Town

and stragglers from that plug-in scene
can't find a match to fire up the furnace

No one gets out of their Coupe de Ville,
none of us sweats the soft-core pages
But test lights flickering

across your brow mean
I've hardened that pharaoh's heart of yours

so you'll never believe this gripping,
panoramic tale of how herons or snakes
can bear souls aloft to market

Then a gate swung through my one-rule mind,
through its rounded, swallowable lock
and my mouth goes lipstruck

down, all dented
from smoke you feel colliding now
An unfinished burning of whatever's saved is

used to blacken my sleeping hand and yours

What changed your line of sight,
steered you toward
this smiler with a knife who punctuates

the spirit job we might do between us?
It's nighttime and we dig around its browned out,
lacquered hours

It's become my living life, the one I'd hoped for

back when I first started to experiment
with the Alleged New Force

That's when I tore up our bed so I might finally
feel some decisive, chemical twitch
But I just wasn't smart enough to look

away when those photos you took of yourself
found their way into my dirty eyes

That's why my *meanwhile* gang rode back,
deliverance wrapped around their shoulders
They will always work my wheels
against yours

and when the hand that works all these
grows tired, then another kiss within me
heaves off on its blind way

toward no one
And the gate swings and the wires hum
and whatever I've done you tell me was done

by me to you before waking

UNGLUED: PINS LEFT IN

In every dwelling, even the richest, the first task of the phenomenologist is to find the original shell. **GASTON BACHELARD** *The Poetics of Space*

Streets papered over. Those houses
they fed, boarded up. We fidget between

fractioned shades. Brick shards, faucet's
ice-glint. *Domus* sheared down to shoe

level, dried out, flaking, ready
to be blown off by newly unpackaged

winds. This is where our falsification
gets its broody shape: an asylum

within what's gone, where tarnished
brass hinges polish up nicely

to gold & rooms that hardly held
their own description now

hold the quick smack of blood
pulsing at the temples, of expectations

unglued. Plastic sheets on windows
bloom like sails, a rusted fork

is driven in one splintered jamb.
With the doorbell nothing more

than free-sprung wires, guests, it seems,
have no choice but to hammer

with whatever's hard, sharp
or handy enough to raise the dust.

HELD, OVER

1

Call so much of this place empty then say the rest gets
so filled up that all
the loudest smoke rises through the floorboards to make
a furnished room out of whatever you find
yourself sitting

& tapering off these days in.
How did you learn to hairsplit every sudden thing,

as flashbulbs flare
madly at your mind and its gathered wings,

yet stitch them back together to save the feel of a headfirst
    plunge?
Things falling fall straight down, no swerving from
themselves, but what's built ends up
shedding

its rock & paint & the skin it piled upon itself from the cellar
to its ceiling,
because what pencils do

to paper
is really nothing more than recitation, than beginning with
& starting at,

a measure of your tendon's imprecision.
And you wonder why we're anxious here, bundled up,
teeth rattling,
chins pressed to our chests

just waiting
for an all-terrain sentence whose predicate rubs hard
enough to bury
us in its erasure.

2

O housetop, housebound world,

some messenger beats at some door.
We were drinking, we were walking & then your foreign
    field's ideation swung onto the scene
willing us

& welding
our heads into a kind of camera that thinks it doesn't need
    light.

A mineral cry
aimed at your macula lutea, its brutal hit a way to bounce
these square-jawed rooms & prove

the eye is only a chemical reaction with sensors plugged
into copper-blue air & our realizing that,

like faucets or like lips around spoons, someone's always
    turning or
something's getting swallowed.

But watch these unpedestalled skies go folding & folding more,
their borders pried open by handheld tools:
a trowel, a synonym, or maybe
this tenor saw now

severing your heat
from the fever you've spilled on this stage.
Surely that's the rough stuff we came for,

windmilling arms colliding, even in the crowdless aisles;
the downdrafts

carrying spit to coffee-cans for storage.

3

We're pinched against walls & we've raised ourselves a
    broken, whisper-laced roof.
The dark, then darkening ground, the feel of which

drifts across your fingertips like breath that's blown
to cool some burn,

lays far below us & sleeps as if hidden by the simple act
of lying down.

What do we see & what exactly is
sight, after it's been smothered by the word's own taste?
It's nothing but our piercing

part, the piece

built out of other parts, the one no different from another,
like a small knob

on a door as big as needed to go out of here & into
    whatever there
there's left.

Guess again.
It's the bring-Down singers come

round to hoot & wail beside
your bed until they pry apart

those lids & tug your sightline
back to the present, Ongoing deal.

The day's all laid out—creamy smooth
as the clock-radio blasts a pitch for *Alarm Me*,

the *Theft-No-More* home alert system
which is really, at this dim hour, an ice-pick

grazing your nape. You just *know*
wiseacres with nose-rings & strange teeth

are out to snatch your best-loved Stuff, then joyride
in a beat-up Nissan, sift

for pawning & dump the rest
in an underpass. Then decent, burglar-Proof

folks, unblinking, can rumble over
your snapshots of handstands in a motel pool,

the sour-milk smelling watchband you hoped
would someday come clean,

& your *Get-Ready-for-Messiah* keychain, as you
cool in your own *chez Empty*'s tumble-weed breeze.

You're not even upright, the last
cacti not Gone from beside that dream butte

that was a pyramid that had been a ship
or a fist or a fist-shaped ship.

No, none of it fully chased off but already
they're waving you in, the motorized

clouds going *ka-chug.* Hugs & all lustrous phases
of Matter await you at yet another finish.

Her bridges burned, she sizes up my need
for supplication to be secretly applied. Watch how
she sews herself in my body's ground & then, fresh
sweat above her lip, she idly fingers the hem
of her dress. What a fetching picture, her face
so thoroughly unlearnt from by any of us.

A smart penance is one that dresses like a choir,
she says. *It's bulletproof.* Such a liquid game
she plays. Instead of sips & dances, we're huddled
over a paper scrap, heads in a twitchy fog. It's just
another map for ushering sighs to detention alley.

She has words with me, then strings them like
party lamps along the patio where she reclines,
swizzle-stick stuck between painted toes. Lofty gods
oscillate above her wicker chaise; they're primed
for spite's emission. I watch as flirty feet
brush dirty ground: I'm her slice of life, buttered up
with her brain's trick blade.

There's some bit of conscience lingering among
these nervy meals. Phone lines crackle with
corkscrew explanations set on *dial madly.*
What a pithy gal, a whiff of beer on her bra strap.
Has any angel ever curled her wings this hard?

And when I say I saw an ark, or a culprit hurled,
she suspects convulsive shuddering. She clocks
my lazy fabrications, then does me
in fits, or in fists, sends me downrange to sleep
by the stove in spiraling ash.

That mind obedient to disorder ruins roundly,
makes nail clippings out of a crescent moon.
She talks about Real Themes, their flowery
stain smearing her mouth & slurring her speech
as she blows a kiss to some wise-ass kid's cock.

So let her gravy train dampen my dust & leave
me muddy-minded. Around my guilty head,
like snow on the brim of a hat, her cast off
homonyms gather: Waste & waist. Break & brake.
As love fumes on thistly lawns, it's dizzy hour
come round for Alfalfa & Darla. When she blinks
I can loosen her eyes from mine, which,
untethered, go swimming, go solemn unto pause.

FILTERINGS

FOR EVE ASCHHEIM

(as we were clued in)

as we removed the partners from their Parallel hides
        Likewise the (fingernail)   parings of partitioned minds:

some of us do our Circuit & do rolling and Overs & all
                                of that blindly,
                                    done beaut-
                                    ifully unconscious of

                        what we lose while barreling dead-
ahead, our egg shell anatomies barely denting the sofa,
        & sucking from orbital air the shadow

given off from   Around an undrawn line.
yet we concentrate: because we do. so effortlessly, you see,
                                lacking in
                                    Ironman squeeze

but instead, being circulatory, like blood, with points
        of departure & Expectation   anywhere, all at once.

(come simmer: sheets unweld)

Consider:
she was held by bodily Shivers, was

draped in transparencies. ⸱   & bundled up
            inside a metal shed as a storm Scattered senseless
                    telegraphy above,

but she Did Not move herself either way; she was as Grounded
                            as she was sharply
                                grooved; bent as she was

taken up by her arms   then
            straightened out from the waist.

(sung shut a song)

hung up among the wax-faced parrots, sewn in
        deep beneath their wicks—you get
                    the glyphic picture, pal—

    i was lathered in matinee clatter, only circus breath
to breathe & my mouth was a single word Screwed together
                    by a clenched hand in

graceless rotation.   i think of us as grass Grown
        souls; i think such thoughts are
                    a kind of incision:

made inside the side, the Soft, milky side
        that bleeds so as to feel.

(these, then those laid down)

trees & the tree-Made town—an Armory
                                    of doused torches. the same
faces that hid before

still hiding.   & Theseus, skin washed slick in feathered rain,
          jogs round the jugular streets
                                    Giving big-hearted waves
                                              to the Cretans.

(let me caper off to find)

let me rewind.   my stalking tape. & wonder how
    many thousands were airlifted, how were
                              the crying Ones
                                  fed & why Sluggo

      pulled the lever to let Nancy slide forever down
              the Shit chute.   our boxing Ring ain't Round?
                              but still

it's like the mind: there's mud & flint & furious Green
            sentences Spilling & staining the mat.   look Out, here

comes a new way of seeming.   over, around, & thru
              the Pale blue zero
    the kid with the boxcutter Cut in your rug. no matter

          which way you move you will end up resembling
                      yourself, minus actual Size & your always
                          revolving mask.

He kept a notebook. To write things down. His Thoughts. His Visions. Insights pried from the life around him. Or at least that was the idea. When, after nearly a year, he read his notebook he found that it offered little in the way of cogent thoughts; its visions were those garbled idiocies afforded by marijuana or too much cough medicine. His thoughts were commonplace, possibly fit for an advice column but otherwise disposable. This mental repository turned out to be a garbage pail—sentence scraps, half-bitten diatribes, stale images, and tangled anecdotes smelling of the confessional. Confused, boring scribbling which he had scrupulously preserved.

The notebook, in short, was an embarrassment. An egregious one. He abandoned the project and turned his attention to getting rid of the evidence. He was afraid to simply throw it out because some neighbor might pluck it from the bin and raise gales of laughter among their friends by reading it aloud. Even though his name was nowhere on the notebook, this unlikely scenario prevented him from just tossing the despised thing in the trash. His ragged prose so stank of his own mind, he couldn't imagine anyone not recognizing the author. The notebook seemed to scream his inner-most name.

It was too thick to safely burn in his apartment, so he ended up taking a wide marker pen and going through the book line by line and blacking out what he had written. This took about three hours and two markers. Yet drowning in ink all of his wind-up ironies and blowhard epiphanies proved a delicious task. As he watched his carefully chosen words slip under the marker's black wave he thought of how sheets are pulled over the dead. When he was done he was head-achy from the smell of the pens but, oddly enough, he was pleased with the resulting object. Page after page of undulat-ing black waves. Flipping through the book made him even dizzier as the heavily striped pages poured down on one an-other. He almost needed to take hold of his desk to steady himself against the feeling that he would fall forward into the book's grated maw.

He decided to do it again. He filled another notebook with sentences copied out of the dictionary and again effaced every word with black marker lines. He did this repeatedly for a few days, using different colored markers, white-out, enamel paint, sealing caulk, nail polish, and Alberto VO5 (it ate at the paper, leaving pages looking like they'd been through the washing machine). Some months later a friend of his at an art gallery put them in a show and they sold for a couple of thousand dollars each.

These days he doesn't write down His Visions and His Thoughts. Whatever small, crumbled tissues of words congeal in his brain, he leaves there. Damp. Piled high. He now believes this is the best way to save it all. Because someday, when it all rots and turns to fertilizer, he may be able to grow something good in there. The kind of thoughts that when you read them you don't want to take a hammer and break the fingers on the hand that bothered to write them down.

All the dogs have had their daily dose,
a haze settles in the blood.

It's time to smoke
out the glittering porcelain

beasts from their curiosity
cabinets & shimmy

up the lookout tree where,
unimpeded, the sun's abraded flesh

can be flayed in that backroom
behind the eyes.

We are guided by blue guides,
blue commands; we configure

a vibratory language from kerosene &
handmade scars,

even as arguments about afterlife versus
infrared night vision tire

our most robust vituperators.
Metallic & slippery, bedtime cocoa

does what's expected—
soon we are hunters in a syrupy

chase through wild grass.
Off in the mudflats, out past

the target range, big loping strides
carry us almost within reach

of our devious, double-minded prey.
The young ones scurry ahead; the rest of us

dote on our graceful escalation
through the zone of storm-bent trees.

Open-mouthed, unmarvelling,
we are as wordless as mighty doom

as we barrel ahead, steam chugging
from the noisy brain

of our Great Forbidder.
Come dawn the syndrome cycles off

& hearts leap at *Big Chew Now*: frosted
flakes beneath an unspooned nimbus.

We idle smoothly, exchanging heat
for heat & unfastening from our guidebooks

the wakeful, roving name
for each of the miles we've dreamt through.

In this they lived and lived almost
all of their years in this,
this house which is really a road
on which weather alights

At first there was something and
then there was less and then even
less and their leftover fruit sat out
and spoiled in the day's own sun

From this they left as if almost alive,
all of their tears on this,
this road that was never a house
on which weather alights

At last there was nothing and
then there was nothing else and then
only their own fruitless days which
spoiled and burst in the leftover sun

Your inner life, with its fist of burnt-up arousal, that's the one you want riding next to you as you move with all available force toward a surprising conclusion which will, even as your hands grip lovingly the wheel, nail you back hard to the seat where staying put is the only way you can suck in even the smell that comes off a verb. But still, you want some inner life.

You need to be known. I know you. You know me too. I've been on the job from the start, from back in the Brownian-motion days when stars were things you only saw when someone stuck their thumb in your eyes. Of course, now it's different. Now we're all regular Joes with our fingers on the Proust button ready to fire. Bend over, art lover. It's your turn to venerate at the wink of an eye.

I was marked with a jaw-wired stammer that kicks in when I hear you pounding with your nightstick at the door. No one reads with their lips quite so tied and twisted as you do when you try me on. You handle me while I sink and sink. It's written out in my Optick Nerve and surely it's written in yours. Yes, somewhere in that fat head of yours is the fierce cog driving this interrogation.

Our statue bled, then smoked an unfiltered Chesterfield. The lasso of smoke around the Virgin's brow prophesied tomorrow's prison. We read the signs: we're readers, that's what readers do. All over town we see red eyes and rope-burned hands telling the same story—soon everyone will be scrambling for their own place at the hungerthon table. I do Braille; you're good at ashes. Fingering the fine stuff. Blackening your thumbs. You've got a mouthful of worldview and an eyeful of spite. And now it's clear: a duct tape job awaits us both.

Me and you, we're such punks. Situationalists ready to ride herd on the punishment crew, if only they promise us candy and clean sheets. We're believers in how, when heaped up in great piles, when the breath of some suffocates all, how living bodies feel to other living bodies no different than if they were heaped up and dead.

Look at us, our lullabies. You believe in ordinary words doing daily chores, in a kernel of truth, the gist of things, the heart of the matter. Me, I'm sweet on the unhinged locale, the sentence city whose borders are so vague they cannot predicate a center. But can we at least agree about the failed rope trick any conversation really is? Before we knot up our clauses, let's be frank: nothing you say and nothing I say, no matter how bravely or pleadingly said, changes the fact that our hearts' scissors have already had the final say and they said, *This rope stays cut.*

ALBERT MOBILIO is the recipient of a Whiting Writers' Award and the 1998 National Book Critics Circle Award for reviewing. His work has appeared in *Harper's*, the *Village Voice*, *Grand Street*, *Bomb*, and the *New York Times Book Review*. His books of poetry include *Bendable Siege* and *The Geographics*. A book of fiction, *The Handbook of Phrenology*, was recently published as a limited edition artist's book (with etchings by Hilary Lorenz). He is the fiction editor at *Bookforum* and teaches writing at New York University.